Enjoy the View!

J Scott Dunham

BLUE RIDGE

PARKWAY PLACES

J SCOTT
GRAHAM

BLUE RIDGE
PARKWAY PLACES

Photography by J. Scott Graham

Design by Jay Huron,
Hillhouse Graphic Design

Created in the USA.
Printed in Malaysia.

ISBN 10: 1-890483-36-2
ISBN 13: 978-1-890483-36-4

jscottgraham.com
(888) 301-9248 *toll free*

title page:
BLACK MOUNTAINS near milemarker 362

MILEMARKERS

Below is a listing of highlights along the Blue Ridge Parkway, designated by milemarker number. Milemarkers are located along the roadway's grassy verge and were first installed in 1947. Designed for maximum long-distance visibility, milemarkers are three-sided, with the number of miles from the northern terminus incised on the two sides angled toward the road.

VIRGINIA

0 Rockfish Gap
6 Humpback Rocks
11 Raven's Roost
19 Twenty Minute Cliff
20 Slacks Overlook/ White Rock Falls
27 Crabtree Falls (exit Hwy 56)
29 Whetstone Ridge
34 Yankee Horse Ridge/ Wigwam Falls
53 Bluff Mountain Tunnel
63 Otter Lake, Otter Dam
64 James River
77 Sunset Field Overlook/ Apple Orchard Falls
83 Fallingwater Cascades
86 Peaks of Otter
115 Roanoke River
116 Virginia's Explore Park
120 Roanoke Mountain
154 Smart View
167 Rocky Knob
176 Mabry Mill
189 Groundhog Mountain
190 Puckett Cabin
194 Orchard Gap
213 Blue Ridge Music Center

NORTH CAROLINA

218 Cumberland Knob
239 Doughton Park
259 Northwest Trading Post
272 E.B. Jeffress Park
293 Moses Cone Park
297 Julian Price Park
304 Linn Cove Viaduct
305 Grandfather Mountain
316 Linville Falls
321 Chestoa View
331 Museum of NC Minerals
339 Crabtree Falls
345 Twin Tunnels
355 Mount Mitchell State Park
361 View Glassmine Falls
365 Craggy Gardens
382 Folk Art Center
384 Blue Ridge Parkway Visitor Center
408 Mount Pisgah
412 Cold Mountain
415 Looking Glass Rock
419 Graveyard Fields
422 Devil's Courthouse
431 Richland Balsam
451 Waterrock Knob
469 Great Smoky Mountains National Park

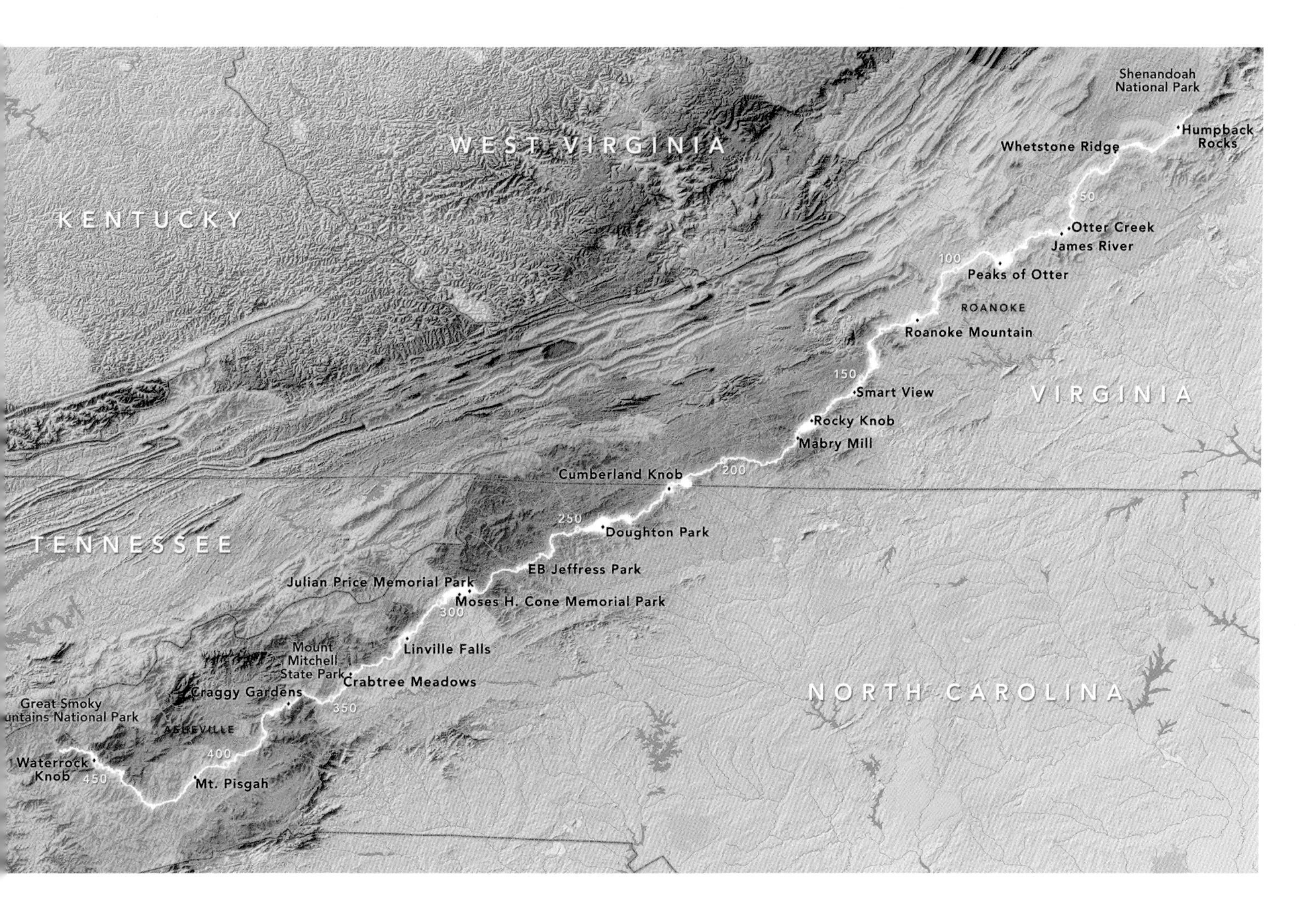

BLUE RIDGE PARKWAY

Blue Ridge Parkway, 199 Hemphill Knob Road, Asheville NC 28803-8686 • (828)271-4779 • www.nps.gov/blri/

Dear Friends,

During the three decades I have been working behind a camera my photographic odysseys have extended from the California coast to the Caribbean rainforest. However, I will always continue to explore the one area closest to my home and to my heart — the Blue Ridge Parkway.

My oldest son is now in college at Clemson and my youngest son has started high school - subtle reminders that time continues to flow by like a gentle mountain stream. The older I get the more I have come to appreciate the opportunities that God lays before me, realizing that those precious moments come and go so quickly, never to be repeated.

I guess that has always been my fascination with photography. It is an art that captures and preserves a single moment in time, a glance at this world that evaporates as quickly as it arrives.

For those who enjoy my images I want to thank you for allowing me to continue my craft. I cannot imagine ever doing anything else, especially with so many beautiful Parkway Places.

J. Scott Graham

Passing over the slopes of RICHLAND BALSAM near milemarker 431, the Blue Ridge Parkway reaches its highest point at an elevation of 6,053 feet.

The **PUCKETT CABIN** near milemarker 190, commemorates Orelena Puckett, a midwife who successfully delivered more than 1,000 babies between 1890 and 1939, when she died at the age of 102.

Aptly named for the numerous large boulders strewn across its surface, **ROUGH RIDGE** runs along the flanks of Grandfather Mountain, and offers sweeping views of the Linn Cove Viaduct and North Carolina High Country near milemarker 303.

A 1.6-mile trail through **GRAVEYARD FIELDS** near milemarker 419 leads upstream along Yellowstone Prong to the base of Upper Falls, while a shorter trail leads downstream to Second Falls.

With its high pastures, miles of post-and-rail fencing, rocky outcrops and dramatic views, 5,410-acre DOUGHTON PARK is the largest parkway recreation area in North Carolina and extends from milemarker 239 to milemarker 245.

According to legend, **DEVIL'S COURTHOUSE** near milemarker 422 was where the devil sat in judgment on all those who lacked courage or had strayed from virtuous conduct.

A 2.6-mile loop trail at Crabtree Meadows near milemarker 339 leads to CRABTREE FALLS, a 60-foot cascade that descends through the peaceful hollow of an oak and hickory forest.

BEAR DEN OVERLOOK near milemarker 323

An overlook near milemarker 361 provides a distant view of 800-foot **GLASSMINE FALLS** as it slides down the rock face of Horse Range Ridge.

Hawksbill is one of several distinctive peaks in **LINVILLE GORGE WILDERNESS**. Accessible near milemarker 317, the eastern rim of Linville Gorge also features Table Rock, Sitting Bear and The Chimneys.

Exiting the parkway near milemarker 412 onto Highway 276 provides access to **LOOKING GLASS CREEK** as it dances through the Pisgah National Forest.

HUMPBACK ROCKS near milemarker 6 is the first contact station for southbound motorists who access the parkway from Skyline Drive or Rockfish Gap. Its most popular feature is a mountain farm exhibit that features a weasel-proof chicken house and a bear-proof hog pen.

At an elevation of 6,684 feet, **MOUNT MITCHELL** is the highest point in the eastern United States and is accessible via a spur road from the Blue Ridge Parkway near milemarker 355.

The 13.5-mile **TANAWHA TRAIL** utilizes several arched bridges and boardwalks designed to blend with, and protect, the fragile ecosystem it passes through. Completed in 1993, this trail is accessible from several overlooks between milemarker 299 and milemarker 305.

LINN COVE VIADUCT near milemarker 304

MABRY MILL, located near milemarker 176, was built by Ed Mabry during the early 20th century. Despite experiencing poor slope and insufficient water supply, Mabry operated the mill to grind cornmeal, saw logs into boards and power a woodworking shop.

After Ed Mabry's death in 1936, **MABRY MILL** fell into disrepair and was nearly destroyed by a state highway crew clearing parkway right-of-way. Instead, under the direction of parkway designer Stan Abbott, the mill was restored in 1942.

CRABTREE FALLS, just off the parkway near milemarker 30, is the highest waterfall in Virginia and is considered by some to be the highest waterfall east of the Mississippi River. The falls drop 1,200 feet over a quarter-mile stretch including one descent of almost 500 feet.

WATERROCK KNOB offers a high elevation view of the Balsam and Great Smoky Mountains from its 6,292-foot summit near milemarker 451.

Near milemarker 364, the parkway passes between Craggy Pinnacle and Craggy Dome, the two dominant peaks in **CRAGGY GARDENS** where heath balds glow pink each June when the Catawba rhododendron bloom.

The centerpiece of Price Park, forty-seven acre **PRICE LAKE** near milemarker 297 is the parkway's largest water feature, and is a favorite location for trout fishing, canoeing, and hiking.

GREEN KNOB OVERLOOK near milemarker 350

Near milemarker 316, the **LINVILLE RIVER** descends over 2,000 feet in a 12-mile stretch as it flows through Linville Gorge, the deepest river gorge in the eastern United States.

With an elevation of 5,946 feet, **GRANDFATHER MOUNTAIN** provides habitat for more globally rare species than any mountain east of the Rockies. Access to Grandfather Mountain State Park requires exiting the parkway onto Highway 221 near milemarker 305.

A stone overlook along the Trail of Trees provides a commanding view of the placid JAMES RIVER as it floats underneath the parkway near milemarker 63.

YONAHLOSSEE OVERLOOK near milemarker 304 provides a sweeping sunrise vista of the Blue Ridge Mountains just north of the Linn Cove Viaduct.

Sixty-foot **LOOKING GLASS FALLS** descends through the Pisgah National Forest in North Carolina's Transylvania County near milemarker 412. This area is known as the "Land of Waterfalls" because it has more waterfalls than any other county in the state.

Though a barn was removed to make way for construction of the parkway, the **BRINEGAR CABIN**, along with a granary, outhouse and springhouse remain in their original locations near milemarker 239 in Doughton Park.

PRICE LAKE near milemarker 297

A spur road near milemarker 316 provides access to a network of hiking trails leading to **LINVILLE FALLS**. Erwins View Overlook provides a panoramic vista of the falls and is reached via a moderate 0.8-mile hiking trail from the visitor center.

Located near milemarker 6, **HUMPBACK ROCKS** is a jagged outcrop one mile up a zigzagging trail that is crowned by spectacular views into Rockfish and Shenandoah Valleys.

E.B. JEFFRESS PARK stretches from milemarker 272 to milemarker 274 and features The Cascades, a waterfall visible along a 0.6-mile trail; a picnic area; and a cluster of historic structures: Cool Springs Baptist Church, the Jesse Brown Cabin and a springhouse.

The 3,875-foot summit of Sharp Top rises above 24-acre Abbott Lake at the **PEAKS OF OTTER**, located near milemarker 86. Hiking trails around the lake provide access to Polly Woods Ordinary, the Johnson Farm, and nearby Fallingwater Cascades.

A steep, 1.6-mile loop trail near milemarker 83 leads to **FALLINGWATER CASCADES**. This waterfall has a series of drops totaling more than 200 feet as it passes through the Jefferson National Forest.

With its signature flat top, **TABLE ROCK** is one of the parkway's most distinctive peaks. Accessible near milemarker 317, this 4,100-foot summit rises along the eastern rim of Linville Gorge which was designated a wilderness area in 1951.

GROUNDHOG MOUNTAIN near milemarker 189

Overflow waters from Otter Lake spill over Otter Dam and into **OTTER CREEK** near milemarker 63 where the parkway reaches its lowest elevation at 649 feet above sea level. This mountain stream parallels the parkway for another 1/2 mile before flowing into the James River.

Located near milemarker 407, **MOUNT PISGAH** was named after the biblical mountain from which Moses saw the Promised Land. An observation platform on the 5,721-foot summit is reached via a 1.5-mile trail.

Twenty-six tunnels were constructed along the 469-mile parkway, including **TWIN TUNNELS** near milemarker 345. Twenty-five of the tunnels are located in North Carolina due to the higher elevations and more rugged peaks of the road's southern section.

Located just off the parkway near milemarker 333 in Little Switzerland, North Carolina, is GRASSY CREEK FALLS. Though this 30-foot waterfall is on private property, the owners have graciously agreed to let hikers access a half-mile trail to the falls.

In 1897, Moses Cone purchased Flat Top Mountain to develop a summer retreat in Blowing Rock, North Carolina, which is now enjoyed as 3,512-acre **MOSES H. CONE MEMORIAL PARK** near milemarker 293.

A 23-room Beaux Arts mansion, Flat Top Manor looks out over 25 miles of gently winding carriage roads leading down to Bass Lake in **MOSES H. CONE MEMORIAL PARK**.

CRAGGY GARDENS near milemarker 364

From the perch of CHESTOA VIEW near milemarker 321, visitors can see Grandfather Mountain, North Cove and the upper reaches of Linville Gorge.

An overlook near milemarker 417 provides a view of 3,969-foot **LOOKING GLASS ROCK**. Named for the way it reflects sunlight when wet or covered by ice, this giant monolith, with a 400-foot granite face, offers some of the area's best rock climbing.

In 1951, John D. Rockefeller Jr. agreed to foot the entire $100,000 bill that purchased 1,100 acres surrounding **LINVILLE FALLS** so this area could become part of the Blue Ridge Parkway near milemarker 316.

POLLY WOODS ORDINARY, located at the Peaks of Otter near milemarker 86, was operated as an inn, or "ordinary," in the mid-1800s by the widowed Polly Woods. Travelers received hot meals, comfortable beds and a stable for their horses.

When the last rays of summer sunlight shone only on **TWENTY MINUTE CLIFF** near milemarker 19, farmers working in the valley below knew they had 20 minutes remaining until sunset.

Situated north of Price Lake, the quiet waters of **SIMS POND** rest just below the parkway near milemarker 296.

CUMBERLAND KNOB near milemarker 218

At an elevation of 4,602 feet, **LICKLOG RIDGE OVERLOOK** near milemarker 349 provides a view of several neighboring mountains as storm clouds clear in the distance.

A half-mile loop trail follows the subtle waters of Falls Creek to **THE CASCADES**, a 250-foot waterfall accessible near mile marker 272 in E.B. Jeffress Park.

A set of steps leading down from Wilson Creek Overlook near milemarker 304 lead to a path that wanders underneath the parkway, then intersects the **TANAWHA TRAIL** near a wooden footbridge.